G is for Georgia

A STATE ALPHABET BOOK

SWEETWATER
PRESS

G is for Georgia
Copyright © 2006 by Sweetwater Press
Produced by Cliff Road Books

ISBN-13: 978-1-58173-524-6
ISBN-10: 1-58173-524-3

Printed in China

G is for Georgia

E.J. Sullivan

Illustrated by Neal Cross

SWEETWATER
PRESS

A is for Atlanta's downtown skyline.

B is for
the Braves
winning
every time.

C is for all the kinds of Coke we adore.

D is for them Dawgs my brother roots for!

E is for eating everything fried.

F is for the Falcons who will always fly high.

G is for all the famous generals from here.

H is for Hank Aaron, best player of any year.

I is for interstates: 75, 85, 95, and 20.

J is for junk sales—
Dad says you can't
have too many.

K is for Dr. King, and what he gave to us all.

L is for Lenox, where Mom shops at the mall.

M is for Macon,
Moultrie, and
Marietta.

N is for NASCAR, may it last forever!

O is for Okefenokee, all dark and steaming.

P is for peaches we eat morning and evening.

R is for Rock City in the corner of the map.

S is for Six Flags, where we go on my birthday.

T is for the traffic that backs up on the beltway.

U is for golf under par,
Grandpa's lifetime wish.

V is for Vidalias cooked in every dish.

W is for how wild we get when it snows.

X is for the spot sister fell on her nose!

Y is for Yes! We love Georgia the best!

From **Z** back to **A**, it tops all the rest!